WALTER L. COOK, Harry Trust professor of preaching and pastoral relations and director of student field work at Bangor Theological Seminary, Maine, has a real knack for talking to youth. This may be because he is the father of two sons, or because of his experiences as a camp counselor and part-time director of Christian education. Whatever the reason, he is able to get and to hold the attention of young people, as evidenced by the popularity of his earlier books, *Meditations for Youth* and *Meeting the Test*.

Everyday Devotions
for Youth

Everyday Devotions
for Youth

WALTER L. COOK

Abingdon Press   NEW YORK   NASHVILLE

EVERYDAY DEVOTIONS FOR YOUTH

Copyright © 1961 by Abingdon Press

Library of Congress Catalog Card Number: 61-11783

Scripture quotations unless otherwise noted are from
the Revised Standard Version of the Bible and are
copyright 1946 and 1952 by the Division of Christian
Education of the National Council of the Churches of
Christ in the U. S. A.

SET UP, PRINTED, AND BOUND BY THE
PARTHENON PRESS, AT NASHVILLE,
TENNESSEE, UNITED STATES OF AMERICA

To

Beatrice and Burpee

Preface

A HIGH-SCHOOL BOY FELT THAT IT WAS TIME TO HAVE the privilege of using the family car, so he coaxed his father to give him driving lessons. With some reluctance the father began the first lesson on the long drive that led from the garage behind the house to the highway. The boy quickly learned to start the car, drive forward, steer acceptably, and even back up.

"Say, Dad, driving's a cinch," he said. "I've got it licked already."

The next day came another lesson; only this time the father told the boy to drive to town. This was something else again. Driving in the yard where he had the path to himself was one thing, driving in traffic was another. After the boy just missed slamming into a car ahead of him that made a sudden left turn, avoided smashing into the rear of a truck that stopped unexpectedly, and escaped hitting a convertible that was parked too far from a curb, he pulled over to the side of the highway. With a worried grin he said to his dad, "If it weren't for those other drivers!"

And if it weren't for all the people we have to live with in this world—some of them at pretty close quarters! If only a Christian could retire to his back yard and live like a hermit, then life would not be so complicated. But Christianity cannot be lived in a backyard, or down-cellar, or up in the attic. It has to be lived on many highways, in many relationships.

The aim of this book is to suggest how young Christians can apply their faith to everyday living, not in a vacuum, but at home, with the neighbors, at school, on a date, on the athletic field, in their social groups, as a citizen, and at church.

WALTER L. COOK

Contents

ON A DATE

ON THE ATHLETIC FIELD

IN THEIR SOCIAL GROUPS

AS A CITIZEN

AT CHURCH

AT HOME

Don't Kill Flies with a Club

Faithful are the wounds of a friend
—Prov. 27:6

IN AN AMERICAN CITY A MAN WAS CHARGED WITH KNOCK-
ing down a policeman. The man defended himself by
saying, "I saw a big bee on his neck above his collar.
I didn't want him to get stung, so I hit the bee as
hard as I could." Which proves that the remedy can
be worse than the disease. Many times we hurt people
when we intend to be helpful. Although we should
not be busybodies in our homes telling other members of the family what is wrong with them, it may
be that sometimes we can drop a hint to a younger
brother or sister that will be useful to them. For example, we might notice that one of them speaks too
sharply to his friends or is bossy and domineering
with them. Perhaps we should speak a word of reproof when we can do so with good will. When we
do it, we must use all the tact and skill we can command. To wound a younger member of the family
because we are clumsy and rough is to take away most
of the value of our counsel. It is always difficult for
anyone to take the criticism of a friend, even though

15

that friend is faithfully trying to help. Can we learn to hit the nail on the head without splitting the wood? Can we learn to say a hard thing in a kindly way?

We confess, O God, how difficult it is for us to speak the helpful but hard word to those we love. We are afraid they will be angry. Give us a deep understanding of the members of our family, and so guide us in living with them that we shall be a blessing to them and not a nuisance. AMEN.

Our Biggest Argument: The Family Car

He who loves money will not be satisfied with money; nor he who loves wealth, with gain.
—*Eccl. 5:10*

THE YOUNGER MEMBERS OF THE FAMILY WERE ARGUING over the family car. One of them got it, but later seemed unhappy about it. "What's the matter?" asked his mother, "You got the car."

"Yes, but everybody else is sore about it. What I wanted was to get the car and have them want me to get it."

To get what we want at the expense of the resentment of others is to win a sour victory. We might just as well lose and join the resenters' club. So many people keep on fooling themselves; they are sure that once they got their hands on what they want, they'll be satisfied. The author of Ecclesiastes knew better. He said that if we love money we'll not be happy with it if we get it. If he lived today he might say the same about many of the things we can see and hear and touch. Take that family car again; we want it, shout for it, tease and argue for it. Suddenly the high brass gives in; it's ours. But if getting what we thought we wanted puts us in the doghouse with the members of the family, we'll be miserable. When our connections with people we love become strained, all victories turn to ashes.

Eternal God, help us to know what we really want from life. Keep us from spending our lives pursuing goals that are empty and dissatisfying. AMEN.

Take Home a Special Thoughtfulness

Pleasant words are like a honeycomb, sweetness to the soul and health to the body.

—*Prov. 16:24*

A NEWSPAPER CARTOON PICTURES A BOY WHO HAS brought home eleven of his friends. It shows him standing in the living room at the foot of a stairway calling to his mother who is apparently working upstairs out of sight: "Hey, Mom, guess who I brought home for dinner." When his mother finally sees all the young people she will have to feed, she may faint. Almost all good mothers encourage their sons to bring home their friends—but probably only a few at a time, and not every day.

We might ask ourselves not whom but what we have been bringing home lately: headaches for mother, problems for father, impatient words for brothers and sisters? What about bringing a gift to our parents? For example, we might bring home special thoughtfulness. To be sure, we may not be able to provide for them either costly or splendid presents. Where could we get money to buy expensive bouquets for our mothers or high-priced fishing gear for our fathers? One of the Proverbs suggests that "pleasant words" could be one offering we might make to those at home. Why not take home a special thoughtfulness

18

in the form of a compliment to our parents? How long has it been since we spoke words of praise to them? We might try it sometime today; probably they will not keel over in surprise.

We ask thee to forgive us, our Father, that so often we take our parents for granted. Remembering how much they do for us every day, help us to let them know by our words, as well as our lives, that we are thankful to them. AMEN.

Are You a Cheerful Receiver?

Each one must do as he has made up his mind, not reluctantly, or under compulsion, for God loves a cheerful giver.

—II Cor. 9:7

TWO BOYS WERE DISCUSSING WHAT THEY GOT FOR CHRISTmas. One said that his father had given him a sport coat. "Good stuff," said the other, "have you worn it?" "Not me," was the answer, "I took it back and changed it for a really high-priced basketball."

Some of us might say, "What a pity!" The boy's father bought the coat in good faith, thinking that his son would like to wear it. The fit was perfect. The

19

color was attractive, although not gaudy; and the father spent time, care, and money in selecting it. So much for the father who did not say a word of protest when his son traded his gift for something else. That father was a cheerful giver.

But what about the boy? His father had learned to *give,* but his son certainly had not learned to *receive.* It is true that Paul, when he wrote to the Christians in Corinth, stressed cheerful giving; this is important. Important too is cheerful receiving. Let us warn ourselves against showing ingratitude and coldness of heart toward those who, out of thoughtfulness and love, have put a present in our hands.

Heavenly Father, teach us the grace of glad receiving. In our faces, in our eyes, may we show a happy response when someone has made a gift to us. In the name of Jesus. AMEN.

Have You Gone Out of Control?

A word fitly spoken is like apples of gold in a setting of silver.

—*Prov. 25:11*

"I'VE LOST CONTROL OF MY SON AND HE'S ONLY SIXTEEN. He's rude to his mother and won't listen to me or talk with me until he gets good and ready. I'm not saying he's vicious and I'd resent anyone calling him a delinquent, but he's unruly and hateful most of the time. What can I do? (Signed) A Frustrated Father." This note was sent to a newspaper columnist who tries to give advice to upset parents.

The situation is out of control in many homes, and there is no magic that will resolve all arguments between fathers and sons, mothers and daughters. But if parents and their teen-agers could at least talk together, they might be on their way to improved relations. Sometimes a son, disturbed about home conditions, will watch for an opportunity to commend or praise his father. He desires to communicate with his father and praise him when he gets a raise at the office, lands a 6½-pound brown trout, or has a triumph on the golf course. Then, there can take place an exchange of ideas. Admiring words from a son will make a real dent in Dad. Home difficulties cannot all be cleared away by talk, but a word of praise might be

21

a good place to begin. "A word fitly spoken is like apples of gold in a setting of silver."

Our Father, show us how to live a Christian life among those we love. In our homes teach us the right words to say, and then give us the willingness to speak them: thoughtful words, helpful words, good-natured words. AMEN.

He Started It

Blessed are those who hunger and thirst for righteousness for they shall be satisfied.

—Matt. 5:6

A FREE-FOR-ALL WAS TAKING PLACE IN THE LIVING ROOM. Finally, the father, who was reading on the porch, tossed his newspaper onto the table and went in to quell the riot. "Jim," he asked, "who started this?" "Well, Dad," said Jim, "it all started when Joe hit me back." Anyone who has tried to settle a living-room battle knows how hard it is to find out how the war began (or who is responsible for it). But if, like Jim, I can't tell how the conflict commenced, I ought to be ready as a Christian to stop it. An armistice must be signed at once, and I should be the first one to put my signature on it. The question is this: How may I muster enough good will to help me start the process of bringing peace to my home? Probably the people who are the best equipped to be peacemakers are those who are dedicated to some great goal and do not want to waste time in carrying on a fight. Jesus once said "Blessed are those who hunger and thirst for righteousness, for they shall be satisfied." When we long for, yearn for, and hunger for righteousness, we shall not let ourselves be led very far into rows and scuffles that take us away from our great goal.

Almighty God, put a seal upon our lips to keep us from speaking hot and angry words that will wound those we love. May we, with thy help, do our part in keeping peace and good will always alive in our homes. Through Jesus Christ our Lord. AMEN.

Be Sure to Dump the Rubbish

Let all bitterness and wrath and anger and clamor and slander be put away from you, and all malice.
—Eph. 4:31

GETTING A WOMAN TO THROW AWAY HER FAVORITE DISH that is cracked is as hard as getting a man to throw away his favorite necktie that is old and spotted with soup stains. It's hard to decide what we ought to keep and what we ought to throw away. We need the knack of using the wastebasket properly.

Many of us keep our grudges and prejudices. There's the wastebasket right beside the desk; better use it. But no, like splintered baseball bats, punctured basketballs, bent fishing poles, and old treadless tires, we can't seem to throw them out. They're old friends; we're afraid we'd be lost without them.

The author of Ephesians gives us a long list of harmful attitudes that we ought to carry to the dump. He says, "Let all bitterness and wrath and anger and clamor and slander be put away from you, and all malice." Cleaning house may mean getting rid of some miserable memories we've been hanging onto for dear life: memories of the time we lost a hot argument, of the day our parents were unreasonable, or the week when an older brother seemed more bully than brother. Stuff these in the trash can and home will be happier.

Almighty God, forgive us when we are soreheads and spoilsports, coddling petty slights and minor injuries. Teach us how to hang onto the useful and discard the worthless. AMEN.

24

WITH THE NEIGHBORS

Putting Up with Other People's Weaknesses

Encourage the faint-hearted, help the weak, be patient with them all.

—*I Thess. 5:14*

WHEN ANYTHING WENT WRONG IN THE JONES HOUSE, Mr. Jones instantly repaired it. He was proud of his talent as a repairman, but his family (and some of the neighbors) thought it was misplaced pride. Articles he fixed came unstuck, or came apart, or just fell over. Once he repaired a cuckoo clock for a neighbor. The first time the clock struck, after his repair job, the cuckoo backed out on the landing and asked what time it was. Clumsy repair work seemed to be a weakness with him, and his family and neighbors seldom asked his help.

Have we learned to be patient with the weaknesses of our friends? In life it is often easy to be friends with clever, gifted, talented people. But it is not so easy to be friends with the slow-pokes, the disorderly, the always-late, and the work-all-day-and-get-nothing-done people. It seems to be the lame tiger that gets abused, the queer chicken that gets pecked, and the awkward

27

boy who gets laughed at. The Bible verse that reads "encourage the faint-hearted, help the weak, be patient with them all," speaks to every Christian about his responsibility toward those who are clumsy, disorganized, and awkward.

Our Father, when our friends try hard to help and only succeed in hindering, keep us from judging them impatiently. Rather, may we be grateful for their good will. Increase our own ability to be useful to those who may need us. AMEN.

The Need to Be Noticed

> *Let each one of you look not only to his own interests, but also to the interests of others.*
> —*Phil. 2:4*

JUST BEFORE GRADUATION A GIRL IN THE SENIOR CLASS in high school got an engagement ring. She wore it to school, but no one noticed it. During the afternoon, when she was sitting talking with her friends, she could no longer hold back her good news. She stood up and said, "How hot it is here. I guess I'll take off my ring."

Well, who can blame her? When something wonderful happens to us, we want everyone to know about it and comment about it. If they do not notice our good fortune, we may use some device to call attention to it. When Paul wrote a letter to his friends in Philippi he said, "Let each one of you look not only to his own interests but also to the interests of others." Honors and triumphs make people happiest when their friends acknowledge them. If we are humble in spirit, we will have clear eyes to see the accomplishments of others. Recognizing the achievements of a friend may spur that person to greater attainments.

O God, keep us from being so self-centered that our own achievements occupy all our thoughts. Take from our eyes the mists of selfishness and envy which can blind us to the fine qualities and accomplishments of others. AMEN.

Nobody Speaks to Me

He who guards his mouth preserves his life.
—Prov. 13:3

TWO HIGH-SCHOOL JUNIORS WERE TALKING. ONE OF them said, "Wouldn't it be wonderful if, for just one

29

day, you could say exactly what you wanted to!" "Yeah," said his friend, "except that next day you wouldn't have anyone to talk to."

Telling 'em off is a barrel of fun—if we're on the giving and not the receiving end, or if we are content to become candidates for the office of "The Least-Popular Person in Town." Our Christian faith does not always oblige us to refrain from plain talk, but it does require that we guard our mouths from speaking unfair and brutal criticism of our neighbors. It is one thing to be honest and frank with an acquaintance; it is another thing to stand on his toes and insult him.

All of us have heard the expression "Button your lip." This rude way of saying "Keep your mouth shut" is a speech we ought to make to our own souls when we are tempted to abuse a companion with words that cut. The writer of Proverbs speaks of guarding our mouths as a way of preserving our lives. He would also have been right if he had said, "He who guards his mouth keeps his friends."

We thank thee, O God, for the gift of speech. Help us to guard this gift as a treasure to be carefully handled and wisely employed. Help us to hold back biting words that we want to use when we are angry.

Instead, show us how to speak words that encourage and inspire. AMEN.

Satisfied Being Half Decent

> *And you shall love the Lord your God with all your heart, and with all your soul, and with all your mind, and with all your strength. You shall love your neighbor as yourself.*
>
> —Mark 12:30, 31

ON EAST SEVENTY-THIRD STREET IN NEW YORK CITY IS A mansion where Joseph Pulitzer spent his last days and died without ever having been in forty-five of its sixty rooms. While he was there, he lived in only one fourth of his house.

This may surprise us until we remember our own weakness for cramped and restricted living. There are books on our library shelves we do not read, scenic nature spots near our home we do not visit, and gracious ways to live and work with people we do not explore. Many of us try to keep God himself at a distance. We would prefer not to know too much about his will for our lives, because he might command us to do things for him and our acquaintances

31

that we are unwilling to do. God does not want us to be *reasonably* generous with others, *moderately* kind, *relatively* thoughtful, *mildly* considerate. He calls upon us to be more than half decent, requiring us to love him and our neighbors with all our heart and soul and mind and strength.

Put within us, O God, a great discontent with our half-hearted loyalty to thee. If there are rooms of the spirit which we have not even visited, keep us dissatisfied with ourselves until we have moved into them. AMEN.

Only Temporarily Delayed

For a righteous man falls seven times, and rises again; but the wicked are overthrown by calamity.
—Prov. 24:16

THE FOLLOWING NOTE APPEARED IN THE PERSONALS column of a western newspaper: "To my sponsors, friends and anyone else it may concern: I regret to state that my climb up Pikes Peak on stilts has been temporarily delayed by a visit to a hospital in Denver. However. . . ."

Are we able to complete the sentence that followed

the "however"? Would this be about right? "However, I'm not quitting; just as soon as I can get back on my stilts, I'm climbing again." We might not admire the calamity-seeker who would attempt to conquer Pikes Peak on stilts, but what persistence, what perseverance! That "however" ought to find its way into our speech as we attempt but often fail to live as Christians among our acquaintances and friends. "Today I lost my temper. However. . . ." "In the game this afternoon I was the world's worst loser. However. . . ."

The writer of Proverbs tells about a man falling seven times. He is saying that the best people make mistakes, that they sin, but that their fall is not the end of them. They fall, but will not stay down; they are delayed, but only temporarily.

Forgive us, our Father, when we spend too much time trying to achieve useless goals. But when our aspirations are worthy ones, keep us from ever abandoning them even when we falter on the way to their accomplishment. AMEN.

Being Honest with the Store Clerk

Lying lips are an abomination to the Lord, but those who act faithfully are his delight.

—Prov. 12:22

FROM A SPORTING-GOODS STORE A MAN STOLE A FISHING reel with a long line on it. He went out the door and down the street without noticing that the line had a hook on its end which caught on the counter. After the thief was gone, a clerk noticed the line leading from the counter to the door and followed it out to the sidewalk, down the street, and into the pocket of the thief. The crooked deeds of people are not often so easily discovered; dishonesty does not always take the form of stealing from a counter. Christian young people surely wouldn't think of stealing a fishing reel, a football, or a pair of skis. But there are many ways of being dishonest besides slipping other people's property into our pockets. For example, how do we react when the cashier in the supermarket accidentally cheats the company he works for and gives back more change on some purchase than he should have? Do we return to him the improper amount of change? It was once said of a person who had a reputation for being straightforward and above-board in all his ways: "He's so honest he can be trusted with uncounted money." Can such a statement be made about us? If it can, then we will be a delight and not a disappointment to the Lord.

Help us, Eternal God, to refrain from dishonest deeds even when we are sure we will not be caught. Keep us trustworthy and dependable at all times. AMEN.

Don't Tear Down the Wrong House

> *Why do you see the speck that is in your brother's eye, but do not notice the log that is in your own eye?*
>
> —*Matt. 7:3*

IN A GOOD-SIZED CITY IN THE U. S. SIX HOUSE WRECKERS showed up at the home of Joseph Collins, removed the roof, most of the upper story, and the front porch before Collins arrived and told them they were tearing down the wrong house. These house wreckers focused their attention on the wrong object, and, in many ways, we make the same kind of mistake. For example, when some of us don't get along with our acquaintances, we may tear them down by criticizing the clothes they wear, the way they walk, and the way they spend their money. We find fault with them, when all the time there is something wrong with us. In a sense, we are tearing down the wrong house.

Once Jesus asked, "Why do you see the speck that is in your brother's eye, but do not notice the log that is in your own eye?" When we are having trouble getting along with classmates, teammates, and roommates, we ought to analyze ourselves carefully. Do we ever ask ourselves, "What is wrong with me that I can't keep my friends?" Instead of attacking others, let us examine ourselves. Today let us look in the mirror and not out the window.

Our Father, make us lenient in our evaluations of others and stern in estimating ourselves. Make us shrewd judges of character—our own character. Teach us not to defend ourselves by attacking others. AMEN.

AT SCHOOL

Teachers Are Not All Scoundrels

Be attentive, that you may gain insight.
—Prov. 4:1

A REFORMED SAFE-CRACKER WAS CALLED UPON BY SOME friends to open a great vault in an emergency. He sandpapered his fingertips until they were sensitive to the highest degree, and then started to turn the knobs on the great safe. He was able to detect the slightest movement of hidden tumblers within the great lock and was successful in opening it.

How sharp is our awareness? How alert are we? Do we stay sensitive to the troubles of others? Think of the teachers with whom we spend many hours in the classroom. Much of our talk may sound as though we think teachers are all scoundrels, or at least our enemies. Let us watch their faces as we see them in the classroom, for faces mirror many things—disappointments, discouragement, heartaches. We are not the only people who have bad days; so do teachers. Does the math teacher show by his manner that something is bothering him? Is the English teacher snappish and irritable this morning? Well, why not? Don't we get that way? Let us keep ourselves sensitive to those who are troubled or worried or discouraged. In the words of the writer of Proverbs let us "be attentive that we may gain insight" into the moods of others.

Keep us, O God, from being unfair to those who teach our classes. Make us slow to condemn or denounce. May we learn to put ourselves in their places, and so gain an understanding of their problems and difficulties. AMEN.

Best-dressed Member of the Class

> *Put on then, as God's chosen ones, holy and blessed, compassion, kindness, lowliness, meekness, and patience.*
>
> —Col. 3:12

TWO HIGH-SCHOOL BOYS WHO WERE NOTED FOR THEIR ability to make humorous remarks met just before a school party. "Don't you think my new suit is a perfect fit?" one of the boys asked the other. "Fit? Why it's a perfect convulsion," came the slam-bang answer. Sometimes a fellow with a little more money than his friends have can spend freely on suits and ties and shoes. Perhaps he gets a reputation for being the best-dressed member of his class.

The Christian should never be careless about the clothes he wears, and the author of the book of Colossians gives us some hints about how to be well-dressed. According to one translation (Goodspeed) he charges his readers: "You must clothe yourself with tenderness of heart, kindness, humility, gentleness and forbearance." To be dressed in these qualities of character is, for the Christian, more important than to have a wardrobe of fifteen suits, twenty pairs of socks, and forty-five neckties. The world of school life is full of gay colors; just look around the classroom any day. Needed most are people whose lives are alight with compassion and kindness to others. Think of the many different lives that we touch every day. We can be a blessing to many of them, if we are wearing the proper clothes of the spirit.

Lord Jesus, forgive us when we are vain and proud of ourselves. May our daily living be filled with kindness and compassion. Show us how to be at our best not so much in outward appearance as in inward grace. AMEN.

41

The Temptation to Look the Other Way

We can confidently say, "The Lord is my helper,
I will not be afraid; what can man do to me?"
                                        —*Heb. 13:6*

YEARS AGO TWO BROTHERS, CHARLES AND HANK, JUMPED
into a railroad sheep car and took a ride. At one station a brakeman discovered them and began kicking
Hank. Charlie could not stand the sight of Hank enduring all the violence, so he jumped out of the door
and crawled under the car to the other side, where he
could not see what was happening to his brother.
When we encounter unpleasantness, there is always a
temptation to look the other way. When we see in-
justice, we grow angry and want to defend the person
who is being unfairly treated. But with this desire
rises another: the wish to stay out of trouble.

When the crowd at school is "riding" an unpopular
classmate, or unjustly criticizing a teacher, or jeering at
the school supervisor of music who is doing the best
he can to organize and train a competent band, we
may feel stirred to step in and defend the accused.
Our mouths are about open to speak the word, when
suddenly we remember that if we say anything we may
get the gang's guns turned on us. So we dodge behind
the car. At such a time our Christian faith should provide us with the spunk to speak up in his defense. The

author of the book of Hebrews has some encouragement for us when we are tempted to run and hide: "The Lord is my helper, I will not be afraid; what can man do to me?"

God of understanding and mercy, forgive us when we are cowards. Help us to be daring when we know we should speak out against partiality and unfairness. Then give us just enough words to say what needs to be said. AMEN.

Nobody Likes a Snob

I bid every one among you not to think of himself more highly than he ought to think.
—*Rom. 12:3*

A GROUP OF FRESHMEN CARRIED A BANNER IN A PARADE celebrating the three-hundredth anniversary of their college. On the banner were the words, "This University Has Waited Three Hundred Years for Us." I wonder how the sophomores of the college swallowed that message. Perhaps those cocky freshmen got a lesson soon afterward. Some of us, perhaps carelessly, have a way of talking about our crowd, our clique, our class, as though we thought that anyone who belonged to another group must be of second-rate value. If we do talk this way, we are sure to be considered snobs, for a snob is a person who regards other people as his inferiors.

We may be forgiven if now and then we lose our tempers and explode into sharp words. Most people will remain our friends even if we get edgy and irritable. But nobody likes a snob. Let us seek to cultivate a friendly bearing so that we shall draw people to us, rather than repel them by our aloof and standoffish manner. Paul the Apostle confronts us with a challenge when he says, "I bid everyone among you not to think of himself more highly than he ought to think." When God made us, he did not arrange any of our bones so that we can gracefully pat ourselves on the back.

Deliver us, O Lord, from falling into the habit of comparing ourselves favorably with other people. Help us to enlarge the circle of our friendship, never showing kindness with an air of superiority. AMEN.

One Way to Keep Our Friends

The hearing ear and the seeing eye, the Lord has made them both.

—*Prov. 20:12*

A HIGH-SCHOOL NEWSPAPER CONTAINED SEVEN RULES FOR making friends: "(1) Have a car. (2) Be polite. (3) Have a car. (4) Be agreeable. (5) Have a car. (6) Be a good listener. (7) Have a car. (Numbers 2, 4, and 6 can be omitted if the car is a red convertible.)" If it does take a car to make friends, it takes more than a car to keep them. Rule Number 6, which emphasizes the need to be a good listener, is just as important in making and keeping friends as having a car. There are too few good listeners these days and far too many gasbags. We all know well the egotist who insists on doing all the talking. Between classes, in front of the school building, waiting for the bell to ring, on the way home from school, he keeps up his blabbing. If we belong in the big-talker class, people will not turn to us when they need a friend. When they are in trouble, they will want someone by their side who knows how to listen. If we are good listeners, we may be a help to discouraged people. A classmate who feels he must spill over to somebody and get something off his mind, may seek us out if he knows we will listen

45

quietly. "The hearing ear" that God gave to us can enable us to be helpful friends.

Grant, O Father, that we may become the kind of people to whom others turn when they are in trouble. Give us understanding hearts, clear minds, and, above all, the gift of sympathetic silence when we are asked to listen to the problems of others. AMEN.

The Man with the Broom

As you did it to one of the least of these my brethren, you did it to me.

—Matt. 25:40

A TELEPHONE COMPANY FOUND THAT THE CALL BOX in one of its telephone booths contained too much money. An investigation revealed that a kindly old lady had been dropping loose change into the box every time she passed the telephone, because, she said, "The poor telephone girls don't get much money, you know." There is a great deal of misplaced kindness in this world, performed by people with good intentions but with little common sense. Do we know how to be intelligently kind? For example, how do we treat the plumber's assistant, the washing-machine repairman, the garbage collector, the night watchman or the janitor of our high school? Such necessary workers have been regarded with contempt because their tasks require no formal education. Often the school janitor, for instance, seems to be, in our minds, just the "fellow with the broom." But no matter how drab or humble his task, or how thin his pay envelope, he does not want our forced friendship or condescension. Our self-conscious politeness he will find repulsive, but consideration and respect he will appreciate. When our Lord, who was himself a carpenter, said, "As you did it to one of the least of these my brethren, you did it to me," he identified himself with every worker who has a lowly job to do.

O God our Father, keep before our eyes the great hunger that people have for kindness and recognition. Give us not only the desire and willingness to be kind, but also the skill to speak the kindly word and perform the helpful deed. AMEN.

Of Jackknives and Slingshots

And you shall do what is right and good in the sight of the Lord.

—Deut. 6:18

A CARTOON IN A MAGAZINE SHOWS A NEW PUPIL BEING introduced to the teacher of the fourth grade. The mother is saying to the teacher, "This is Reginald— good luck and God bless you." After a glance at Reginald you are sure that the teacher needs someone to wish her luck, for her new pupil is clutching a slingshot in one hand and an opened jackknife in the other.

In imagination you can see Reginald using his knife to carve his initials on his desk, and the slingshot to pop out windows. All this, of course, is to take place behind the teacher's back.

Perhaps someday Reggie will develop respect for the property of others. Right now he probably has none. Others of us, much older than he, still need to respect public property. For example, some school buildings take a beating because, well, they belong to somebody else. Some young people feel that as long as they are not detected abusing school property, then let that building learn to take care of itself. But if carelessness and litterbugging and scuffing are not always discovered by the authorities, they are known to God, for even our everyday living is known to our Creator. Since we live always in the presence of God, let us resolve "to do what is right and good" in his sight.

Make us more sharply aware of thee, O God, so that all our living which comes under thy watchful eye shall have thy blessing and favor. AMEN.

ON A DATE

No Forced Growth in Real Friendship

In the morning it flourishes and is renewed; in the evening it fades and withers.

—*Ps. 90:6*

TOADSTOOLS COME UP WITH A RUSH. A COUPLE OF DAMP nights and behold, you have a full-grown plant. But its bulk has come too swiftly—at the expense of true strength. See how fragile it is; a kick with the foot and it is crushed. Just try kicking an oak tree which has been growing for thirty years. My aching foot! Gradual growth is needed for many of the finest things in life. Kreisler required time to develop his skill. The painting genius of Rembrandt could not be hurried. The philosopher Kierkegaard used a lifetime of reflection to bring his thought to its greatest conclusions. Even Jesus was thirty before he began his ministry.

If gradual growth is needed to develop skills and talents, it is also needed to permit friendships to mature. For example, friendship between a young man and a young woman needs time to ripen. The kind of love which springs up and flourishes after two evenings of moonlight may die when the moon goes

down. Weeks, and even months, may be required before two people discover whether their interests, stand-
ards, and principles are sufficiently similar to make a
lasting friendship possible. The psalmist speaks of
grass flourishing in the morning and withering in
the evening. Some friendships which grow swiftly may
as swiftly fade.

*O Lord, make clear our vision so that we may not be
overwhelmed or bewitched by surface appeal and
charm. May we experience the joy that can come to
us through deep and enduring friendships.* AMEN.

Something Good to Remember

> *Great peace have those who love thy law.*
> —*Ps. 119:165*

A MOTORIST KEPT LOOKING IN HIS REAR-VIEW MIRROR,
wondering why a light truck was following him so
closely. Finally he discovered that the truck had no
driver but had been hooked to his bumper since he
backed into it in a parking space. Sometimes, events
in our past follow us so closely that we seem to be
unable to escape them. Memories have a way of hook-
ing onto our minds and not letting go. We do not

need to look in our rear-view mirror—our past—to find them. They seem to find us and just hang on. We wish we could uncouple some memories and drive off without them. As the writer of the 119th psalm found peace in God's law, so we, in order to have happy memories tomorrow, must engage in right living today.

Many people have been unable to forget the mistakes they made as young people. They wish they had more good things to remember. Memories can haunt: the memory of a time when we did not fully respect the chastity of the person we were going with, the memory of impure moments, the memory of a date when we permitted an overwhelming passion to take over the evening. Once a girl told her father about a wholesome date she had with a boy, a date that brought no haunting aftermath of regret. She said, "We had the kind of time you don't have to write in a diary to remember."

God give us the drive to use our lives to the full. But may they be controlled and directed by thee, so that if we live a hundred years, we shall not be followed by memories that harass and sadden us. AMEN.

How to Tell a Lie

> *Every sound tree bears good fruit, but the bad tree bears evil fruit.*
>
> —*Matt. 7:17*

A TIRE COMPANY INCLUDED THIS HEADING OVER ONE OF its advertisements: "How to Tell a Lie." When I read the advertisement, I found that the company was not giving out information on how to successfully deceive people. Instead, it told about a machine which could distinguish between good and bad rubber; it could help people to know a lie when they saw one. It is important that we trust people who are our close friends; we must be able to know that we can rely upon them. How safe and secure we feel when we know that our companion's word is always trustworthy! The relationship between a boy and a girl who are often companions must be based upon mutual trust. Since no machine has been invented which can "tell" a lie from the truth, how shall we find out if our acquaintance who wants to become a friend is truthful in all things?

There is a verse in the book of Matthew which might serve as a guide: "Every sound tree bears good fruit, but the bad tree bears evil fruit." Time is needed for a tree to bear fruit, and time is needed for us to know our acquaintances thoroughly. On the one hand, we should not make snap judgments about the characters of people, but, on the other hand, we should not be misled into undeserved trustfulness. In time, our words and deeds will reveal our true selves to people, and theirs to us.

O God, let no untruthful word pass the gateway of our lips. May we require of ourselves the same honesty in word and deed that we expect of others. AMEN.

Are You Willing to Apologize?

He shall make restitution.
—Exod. 22:3

A SKYWRITER TOOK THE WRONG TURN IN HIS PLANE AND garbled the telephone number in the advertisement he was writing in the sky. Calls came in to the wrong number, and the next day the pilot had to take up his plane and rewrite the advertisement, this time displaying the correct number.

Are we willing to go back and do our best to correct the blunders we make? Perhaps on the last date we had, we spoke sharp or discourteous words to our partner of the evening. For awhile we forgot that the kind consideration which is called for at school and in church is just as necessary when we are with a companion. And did we apologize, or was the whole evening spoiled because we stubbornly drew back into a shell and would not admit that we were wrong? Once Moses told the people of Israel that when they did wrong they must make restitution. It is perhaps beyond our powers to make complete reparation when we have stamped on the feelings of a friend. The question is: Are we willing to try to repair the damage? Can we say to the person we have hurt: "I'm sorry. I apologize"? Some people seem to have a hard time saying just the words "I was wrong." Many a broken friendship could be mended if the one who spoke thoughtlessly would sincerely say, "I'm sorry."

We confess to thee, O God, that too often we are not sorry for the damage we do to our friends. We say they deserved what they got. Turn us away from our stubbornness and help us to confess our faults. In thy great wisdom, O Father, show us how to correct our mistakes and make amends for our thoughtlessness. AMEN.

If You Know You're Homely

A glad heart makes a cheerful countenance.
—Prov. 15:13

"Paint me as i am, warts and all," oliver cromwell once said to an artist. It is reported that Cromwell was not a handsome man, but at least he was honest and apparently believed that the truth would do his portrait more good than a dishonest gloss. Many people who are conscious of being homely feel that they are handicapped. They wish they were handsome or beautiful. They discover a new mole with consternation and a new freckle with alarm. The homely boy looks into the mirror at his big nose, his pimples, and his stuck-out ears, and decides he won't ask a girl for a date. After several thorough consultations with the bathroom mirror, he may conclude that he doesn't like girls anyway.

The writer of Proverbs gives some exciting encouragement to homely people, by saying that a glad heart makes a cheerful countenance. If inside us we are cheerful and thankful to God for his blessings, then our faces will show these inner feelings. In their discouragement many plain people have forgotten that a homely face with a happy expression will be better received through the years than a handsome face which shows a melancholy disposition.

Help us, O Lord, to be honest with ourselves without becoming hopeless. If the reflections we see in the mirror are discouraging ones, then help us to compensate for an outer plainness with an inner attractiveness. AMEN.

The Case of the Mimeographed Love Letters

He who is slow to anger is better than the mighty, and he who rules his spirit than he who takes a city.
—*Prov. 16:32*

TWO HIGH-SCHOOL SENIORS—A BOY AND A GIRL—HAD A quarrel. They had been enjoying each other's companionship for several months, but now their friendship was broken. The boy completely lost his temper; the afternoon of the quarrel, to get revenge, he mimeographed all the letters the girl had written to him and distributed them to her classmates at school.

When we lose our self-control, some of us are capable of dirty tricks. Anger can be an awful thing, driving us to deeds for which we will be sorry later. If the boy who passed out copies of the girl's letters was good for anything, he came to a time when he was bitterly ashamed of himself. The writer of Proverbs in many different ways praises the man who knows how to control himself. He says, "He who is slow to anger is better than the mighty, and he who rules his spirit than he who takes a city." A general capable of winning a battle by great skill might later lose what he had won, because he could not restrain his temper. Have we, through a temper tantrum, done and said things which later brought us shame and remorse? Let us ask God to help us rule our spirits when we feel ready to explode.

Almighty Father, show us how we may become rulers of our spirits. With thy help may we learn to resist the temptation to give vent to words and deeds that will bring harm to others and regrets to ourselves. AMEN.

The High Cost of Loving

Many waters cannot quench love, neither can floods drown it.

—*Song of S. 8:7*

JIM WAS PLANNING TO BRING HIS GIRL HOME FROM college to Sunday dinner. He was excited about her

61

and wanted his mother and father to share his enthusiasm. Also, he wanted to make a good impression on the girl. "Jim wants us to make a few improvements around here before Sunday," his mother said to his father. "He wants us to paint the house, redecorate the living room, and buy a new car." It surely costs money to be in love.

To love someone means paying a high price in other ways. For one thing, we must learn to keep our temper; there must be a willingness on our part to keep the lid on explosions of hateful and spiteful words. It costs a lot to put our loved one first and ourselves last. Obligations of loyalty and faithfulness also carry a high price tag.

Before we permit ourselves to fall in love, we might put this question to our own hearts: "Am I prepared to pay the high cost of loving someone?" When we are willing to pay the price to unselfishly love someone, we will be ready to experience an emotion that cannot be quenched by waters or drowned by floods.

Grant, Our Father, that sometime in our lives we may love deeply—so deeply that no price will be too high to pay for such a love. Ever deliver us from shallow desire which does not demand the most and the best of us. AMEN.

ON THE ATHLETIC FIELD

The Folly of Feeling Big

I bid every one among you not to think of himself more highly than he ought to think.

—Rom. 12:3

"I USED TO BE AWFULLY CONCEITED, BUT THE COACH straightened me out, and now I'm one of the nicest guys on the team." So! We wonder whether this newly found humility was noticed by the other members of the squad. "Nice guys" don't usually advertise themselves so enthusiastically.

Although this athlete was noisy in his pride, not everyone who is conceited shouts his arrogance. There are those who are quietly conceited. It is possible to be vain without bellowing about it, and smug without broadcasting it. Noiseless self-satisfaction would bring a reproof from Paul, who warned the Roman Christians not to *think* of themselves more highly than they ought to think. What is our quiet opinion of ourselves? If we feel superior to others because of a few minor victories which drew cheers from our friends, then let us compare our little stack of medals with the trophy shelf of some big-time winner. This may help to deliver us from the folly of feeling big.

65

Eternal God, keep us from becoming vain about ourselves and disdainful of others. Put in us a humble spirit so that thou canst teach and guide us. Help us always to view our own small accomplishments with modesty. AMEN.

What Color Do You Think In?

> *Jealousy is cruel as the grave. Its flashes are flashes of fire.*
>
> —*Song of S. 8:6*

THINK OF HOW MANY TIMES WE EXPRESS OUR MOODS and thoughts in colors. Blue is the color we speak of when we are down-in-the-mouth. We say, "I feel blue." Blue music is sad music. Black often suggests sorrow and evil; we speak of black thoughts or of a black heart. Yellow sometimes stands for cowardice. "He's got a yellow streak down his back," we say. White is an honorable color. A bride wears white, and, to many of us, it stands for purity. Green is the jealous color. We talk about the green-eyed monster or comment that some friend turned green with envy.

There are many contests in everyday living and we cannot win them all. Often we see that some competitor has beaten us, that he has chalked up more points than we have, or that he had skills which got him on the varsity while we have to sit among the substitutes. Some of us are dismayed because an acquaintance has a charm about him which brings to him a popularity we can never experience. Looking at his shining achievements, we are cast down when we see that our own talents seem to have been trimmed to almost nothing. It is then that we start thinking green. And jealousy may burn like a fire within us. It is right then that our Christian faith is put to the test: Can we with God's help cleanse our hearts of spitefulness, hatred, and envy?

Our Father, if we are displaced by a rival who is more gifted than we are, keep our hearts free from jealousy and envy. If we get hurt, may we bear the pain without being spiteful. AMEN.

Kill the Umpire

> *Prove me, O Lord, and try me; test my heart and my mind.*
>
> —*Ps. 26:2*

THE VILLAIN OF THE EVENING HAD BEEN THE UMPIRE who had made some raw decisions. At least an outfielder on a sand-lot league team thought he had. After the game he hunted down the luckless fellow and said politely, "It was really a good game, Mr. Umpire; I'm sure sorry you didn't get to see it."

In a baseball game, or any kind of game, some players get so carried away with the will to win that their eyes get cloudy when it comes to close decisions. A centerfielder has been defined as a player standing a couple of hundred feet away from the plate who can see better than the umpire standing five feet away. But can he really? Is not the player's sense of fairness slanted a little? We clamor for an umpire to be fair, sometimes forgetting, in our zest to win, that fair play should be expected of us too. An umpire or referee in any game must make scores of decisions, some of which may go against us. Are *we* fair when we howl over some decision made in good faith by a referee? Let us test ourselves and ask, "Am I so crazy to win that I often become biased and prejudiced?"

God of justice, in the heat of competition, and even when we fiercely want to win, help us to be impartial and reasonable. May there ever be a place for the spirit of Christ in all our contests. In his name. AMEN.

Pitching Out Self-Pity

Thou has made him little less than God, and dost crown him with glory and honor.

—Ps. 8:5

A CONFERENCE WAS TO BE HELD IN THE COACH'S OFFICE in the high-school building. Good Loser, Big Effort, Cooperation, Try Hard, and Team Play walked in. They all took their places in chairs near the coach's desk. Nobody paid attention to another fellow who came sneaking in. When he sat down, the others moved away from him. The name on the back of his chair was Self-Pity. Being sorry for ourselves makes us unpleasant companions; it is no wonder that everyone gives us a wide berth when we begin to moan about our bad luck. Nobody wants to hear us whine that we've never gotten a fair chance, and that we would make the major leagues, if only we could get a few breaks.

Much of our self-pity comes from envying other people; we wish we had their prowess on the track or on the playing field. We place the shining abilities of some competitor alongside our wooden talents, and then we complain that we have been cheated. The man who wrote the eighth psalm would say to me when I start feeling sorry for myself: "Stand on your feet, man. You are made a little less than God. Stop pitying yourself and remember what God has done for you."

O Lord, keep us from being twisted and warped by self-pity. May we never forget that thou hast made us, and that through Jesus Christ we are thy sons. AMEN.

Is What You Have Worth Protecting?

Every word of God proves true; he is a shield to those who take refuge in Him.

—*Prov. 30:5*

ONCE A MAN WAS ARRESTED IN CALIFORNIA FOR CARRYing a sawed-off shotgun inside his jacket. He tried—unsuccessfully—to make the police believe that he needed the weapon to protect his bank roll of seven dollars. We might think it strange that such a powerful weapon was needed to protect so flat a pocketbook. Yet many of us try to guard at least one useless possession as though it were priceless. That possession is our pride—pride that we won a prize in some contest, that we passed an exam that others flunked, that we came in first in some race. These minor triumphs gave us pride and this pride must be protected at all costs. But is the pride that we have worth protecting?

Does not pride do us more harm than good? It puts us on guard all the time and we begin to feel insecure the moment a rival challenges our abilities. It makes us difficult to live with for we are afraid of people—afraid they will criticize us. We don't like the coach when he tries to offer suggestions for our improvement, and we resent our teammates if they give us even a little advice. The writer of Proverbs speaks of God being our shield if we take our refuge in him. How much better it is to trust in him than to try to defend ourselves.

Take away, O Lord, our foolish pride which makes us feel insecure and fearful of others. May we humbly come to depend upon thee, and not upon anything found in ourselves. AMEN.

Sharing in Another's Victory

Rejoice with me, for I have found my sheep which was lost.

—*Luke 15:6*

"HE IS A LEADER, AND AN EXCELLENT ATHLETE. HE GETS along well with his teammates, but he has one great failing; he is not able to appreciate the achievements

71

of others." This was the report of a basketball coach to the guidance director of a high school.

Is it hard for us to applaud the success of others? Can we congratulate a teammate when he wins a victory, shaking his hand and praising him for a grand performance? We may try with all our might to be pleased when a fellow player gets the cheers, but still find that our words of praise stick in our throat. It is a happy picture which Jesus gives us in the Gospel of Luke, when he tells about a man whose neighbors rejoiced at his good fortune in finding his lost sheep. Someone has said that it isn't necessary to blow out your neighbor's light in order to let your own light shine. We ought to be pleased with the success of others without feeling that we have been cheated ourselves. To try to be a good leader and a crack athlete are not enough; we should go beyond these aims and be sympathetic to the hopes and dreams of others, rejoice in their successes, be pleased with their achievements, and even be sorry for their failures.

Almighty Father, grant us help and strength to be generous and free hearted. Give to us greatness of spirit, that we shall be glad about the achievements of friends and even of our rivals. AMEN.

Getting on Top of Your Temper

A soft answer turns away wrath.
—Prov. 15:1

AFTER BEING ATTACKED AND SUFFERING TWO BLACK EYES and a broken leg, a man was asked if he wanted to prefer charges against his assailant. "No," he said, "he's a friend of mine." This little story appeared in a national news magazine and the name of the man is listed. I'd like to meet him, and if he didn't live 2,500 miles from my home in Bangor, Maine, I'd look him up. Any man who can sit on his temper the way he did is worth knowing.

Many of the people we know just don't make gentle responses when they have been thrashed. Coming close to home, do *we* give soft answers to insults and blows? Somebody slams us and we slam back—that's the pattern we know about, all too well. But when an injured man rolls with the punch and calls his attacker "friend," then we want to stand up and salute him. His patient disposition is needed on the diamond, gridiron, and basketball court, where fierce competition often lights the fuse of exploding tempers. When some rival has roughly handled us and decisively beaten us, can we emerge from the battle and say, "He's a friend of mine"? Forbearance is no pill that one may take in an easy gulp. But God can give us

73

the grace to learn how to turn away wrath with a soft answer.

O thou who canst show us how to rule our spirits, help us when resentment and anger threaten to overwhelm us. Steady us, give us poise, and steel us against giving in to explosions of temper. AMEN.

IN THEIR SOCIAL GROUPS

The Monkey on the Committee

Whatever your hands find to do, do it with your might.

—*Eccl. 9:10*

WE GO TO THE ZOO TO BE AMUSED. SUPPOSE THAT THE animals, wanting to be amused, were to come to watch *us*. Where would they find us at our funniest? Well, why not invite them to a committee meeting? Besides being amused, the animals might find that they were looking into a mirror.

The bear would see himself as he watched some committee member hugging a grievance. Instead of dropping a grudge, he is giving it a bear hug. He thinks he can defend himself that way. The rhinoceros would discover his counterpart. He's the tough-hided fellow who spouts crude remarks in meetings and is so thick-skinned that he never cringes when another member tries to put him in his place. No committee would be complete without a tiger—always snarling. He's the short-tempered fellow. Let another committee-man disagree with him and he'll bare his fangs. There'll be a monkey on most committees who just can't settle down to work. He can't sit still long enough

77

to consider important business. Serious deliberation is called for—and he has to scratch.

At least there would be a beaver present. Thank heaven for the beaver—he's eager to get to work. He dives into the thick of things and comes up with a finished product. Maybe the author of Ecclesiastes thought of the beaver when he wrote: "Whatever your hands find to do, do it with your might."

Whenever we are working in thy name, O Lord, keep us from ill will, crudeness, bad temper, and foolishness. AMEN.

Don't Be a Broken Record

Lift up your eyes, and look from the place where you are.

—Gen. 13:14

PRINTED IN A NEWSPAPER WAS THE FOLLOWING ADVERtisement: "For Sale. Just in time for Christmas, a set of records that teen-agers will be crazy about. Some of these records are slightly broken . . . slightly broken . . . slightly broken . . . slightly broken. . . ."

In your club perhaps there is someone who harps on the same theme until everyone gets sick of him.

When he rises to say something during a business meeting, everyone cringes and groans. "Here he goes again," you may say. "Same old wet blanket, same old hopelessness, same old complaints." When a new project is proposed and everyone else is enthusiastic about it, that "sad sack" of a pessimist is sure to be on his feet sounding like a broken record: "It won't work . . . It won't work . . . It won't work . . . It won't work."

In all of us there is a tendency to repeat our pet peeves, so that our friends know just about what we are going to say when we open our mouths. In working with other people we need to stretch our vision a little. Like Abraham of old, who may have felt he was getting into a rut, we would do well to lift up our eyes and look from the place where we are. It may be that God will open our eyes to some new land we can conquer for him.

Father in heaven, help us to be at least a little unpredictable. If we have the habit of responding helplessly and hopelessly to new challenges, show us how to change. Teach us to lift up our eyes to new horizons. AMEN.

Making the Most of Our Mistakes

They who wait for the Lord shall renew their strength.

—Isa. 40:31

WHILE CUTTING THE GRASS IN HIS YARD ONE MORNING, A man got his foot caught in his power mower. His wife drove him to a hospital, where a doctor patched him up and sent him home as good as new. During the afternoon he showed up at another hospital with his other foot damaged—by his power mower. Luckily, he had but two feet to give to the cause! Although some people seem to be unable to profit from their mistakes, others do their best learning on the basis of past blunders. As a tree is fertilized by its own broken branches and fallen leaves, so we may profit from our own mistakes. We may remember a time when we unfairly criticized the chairman of a committee of which we were a member. When we spoke sharply, we blundered and we knew it. We crudely disregarded his feelings. To go on and on making cutting remarks to our fellow workers is unforgiveable. Rather, let us use our past errors as guides to future growth. Isaiah encourages us by saying, "They who wait for the Lord shall renew their strength." In this verse he assures us that God's strength can help us in our weaknesses. God will show us how to benefit from our mistakes, and will teach us to be thoughtful and considerate of others.

Keep us from repeating our failures, O God. Help us not only to confess our faults but also to strive to correct them. Show us how to renew our strength as we meet our daily temptations. In the name of Christ. AMEN.

On Becoming Easier to Get Along With

Let your speech always be gracious.
—*Col. 4:6*

A HIGH-SCHOOL BOY WAS NOTED FOR BEING DISAGREEABLE and unfriendly. One evening he went to a youth meeting in his church and announced that from then on he was going to get along with everybody. Said one of the members of the group, who knew him well, "Man, you'd just better get along with *somebody*." Some people mingle skillfully with their acquaintances in their clubs or social groups; others find it hard to get along with anybody. Perhaps, we feel, we have an unpleasant disposition. We have a face that seems to scowl—we wish we had a sunshiney countenance. We may look sober or grim—we wish we could remember to smile all the time. It is true that our dispositions are judged to some extent by our facial expressions, but, chiefly, people make up their minds about us by what we say and how we say it. If we are known as being fretful and ill-humored, the author of the book of Ephesians has some counsel for us: "Let your speech be always gracious." Almost always a waspish disposition and an irritable manner are communicated to others through our speech. If we learn to put a damper on our tongue when we are tempted to speak sulky or peevish words, we have gone a long way toward becoming easier to live with.

O Lord, if making friends is hard for us, or if we have disturbances with about everybody we know, may we humbly seek the cause within ourselves. Help us to restrain resentful and vindictive words and to replace them with thoughtful and gracious words. AMEN.

Meeting Yourself at a Party

Rejoice, O young man, in your youth, and let your heart cheer you in the days of your youth.

—*Eccl. 11:9*

IN AN AMERICAN HOME THERE IS A FULL-LENGTH MIRROR just inside the front door, where every visitor is sure to see himself as he enters. Whenever young people come to this home, they are confronted by the mirror the moment they open the door. They not only meet their host or hostess, they meet themselves and see the expressions on their own faces. Some dismal moods have been revealed in this mirror. The boy whose girl came to a party with another fellow saw just how woe-begone he looked; so did the chap who had been carrying a grouch all day and hadn't gotten rid of it when he came to the party. A girl arrived for a party one night who thought her hairdo was a mess, and her fretful face greeted her just inside the door. The people who live in this home say that the mirror has helped to bring about some amazing facial transformations.

When we meet ourselves at a party, are we glad we met? The author of Ecclesiastes has many sad things to say to his readers, but occasionally he sounds a happier note, as he does when he says, "Let your heart cheer you in the days of your youth." Let us hold up an imaginary mirror before our faces each time we attend any kind of social. Does our expression show that we have a cheerful heart?

Grant, O God, that thou wilt keep us from denying ourselves friends because we indulge in dismal moods and crabby thoughts. Although we cannot all have handsome faces, we pray that thou wilt help us to have cheerful ones. AMEN.

Packing Off Your Peeves

> *But one thing I do, forgetting what lies behind and straining forward to what lies ahead.*
>
> —*Phil. 3:13*

MANY OF THE WOUNDS WE SUFFER FROM FRIENDS ARE like some insect stings: they're only .03125 of an inch long and the rest is imagination. Someone speaks sharply to us, calls attention to a failing of ours, criticizes the way we spoke up in a committee meeting, or comments on our speckled complexion—and we get peeved. Imagination is a good thing in many ways, but it becomes dangerous when we let it magnify the little digs or thoughtless comments of our friends. Slight injuries to our egos can arouse peeves in us which may be carried for a lifetime.

Happy is the Christian who can pack *off* a peeve—and not pack it *up* to carry with him like luggage, or pack it *away* where it will be kept in the attic of memory. Every peeve that troubles us should have the same mailing address: the furnace, the dump, or the incinerator. Perhaps when Paul resolved to forget "those things which are behind," he was referring to some ugly little memories that he was packing off forever.

Heavenly Father, puncture our self-importance, and let the air out of our inflated egos. When thoughtless comments and unkind words come to us from our acquaintances, give us the grace to forget them. AMEN.

Should Have Kept My Big Mouth Shut

Set a guard over my mouth, O Lord.
—Ps. 141:3

IN ABILENE, TEXAS, A TRAFFIC OFFICER SAW A CAR BEING driven backwards several blocks. He stopped the car and found three coeds who said they had borrowed a boy friend's car, had driven it farther than they planned to, and were now driving it in reverse to back some of the mileage off the speedometer.

Do we sometimes wish we could back some of the mileage off our conversation? Perhaps the last time our crowd got together, we knew we talked too much. We criticized some of our acquaintances who were not present to defend themselves, we made some cutting remarks to one of the others, and we let it be known that just about everybody was out of step but us. The fact is, our tongue broke the speed limit, went through some dangerous intersections, and paid no attention to a stop light. Oh, we wish we hadn't! And now—inside us, at least—we're ashamed. The next time we're out with the crowd, we might remember the words of the Psalmist, and say to ourselves, "Set a guard over my mouth, O Lord."

Forgive us, our Father, when we make fools of ourselves. Help us to remember that the fellow who is always giving others a piece of his mind is usually the one who can least afford it. AMEN.

AS A CITIZEN

Your Town Can Have a Sky Line Too

Whoever would be great among you must be your servant.

—Matt. 20:26

IF YOU HAVE BEEN TO NEW YORK CITY, PROBABLY YOU have noticed that the main street of your town has little in common with Times Square. Perhaps you shot up the elevators in the Empire State Building until you were 102 stories in the air. Can you discover a single building in your "metropolis" that rises more than a dozen stories, or even five stories? Much of the sky line in my home state of Maine is formed not of man-made buildings but of God-made mountains. After climbing Mount Katahdin (our highest) eight times, I found that it differs from most skyscrapers— no elevator.

A sky line need not be made up of buildings and mountains; it can be composed of tall people. Therefore, the smallest hamlet in the United States may have a sky line, if the people in it are great enough in character. Jesus gave a clue in one of his talks about how to be a tall person. He said, "Whoever would be great among you must be in your servant." Are we willing to undertake lowly positions of responsibility in the town in which we live? In our youth we may not be called upon to render many services as citizens of our community, but right now we may grow in righteousness and wisdom. The day will come when we can be citizens who serve, if we have grown tall enough in honor and in ability to be useful.

Show us, O God, how we may become tall in honor and in willingness to serve. May all our thoughts and desires contribute to building in us the kind of character that will be useful to the world in which we are going to live. AMEN.

Thank You, Mister Councilmun

Praise befits the upright.
—Ps. 33:1

"DEAR MISTER COUNCILMUN: THANKS FOR THE CIRKUS ticket, you oughta see the clown. he is a big guy. he played put out the fire. I liked the ellefants. boy you're a swell guy, Mister Councilmun." This is a copy of a note that a member of a city council received from a youngster who had been given a ticket to a circus performance. Perhaps he was the only member who received a thank-you note, although many tickets had been distributed. Why did the "councilmun" so treasure this misspelled, clumsily written letter that he read it aloud at the next council meeting? Perhaps it was because this boy did something unusual; he expressed his thanks. So often we hear about double-dealing and graft at "City Hall"; so seldom do we hear words of praise for those who represent us in civic affairs. To be sure, many of them are paid officials, but no matter how large a salary they receive, every one of them would be gratified if sometimes we, the public, would do as the little boy did: write, or at least speak, our appreciation. In hundreds of ways our elected representatives serve us. Most of them are public-spirited men who should receive our gratitude. When our officials are upright we should praise them.

We thank thee, Our Father, for the public-spirited men who give their services on our behalf. We pray that we may be as ready to praise as we are to blame them, and as ready to appreciate as to criticize. AMEN.

Stopped by a Cop

> *Let every person be subject to the governing authorities.*
>
> —*Rom. 13:1*

OVER THE ENTRANCE OF A TRAFFIC COURT IN MEMPHIS, Tennessee, appears the following sign: "Why Complain? Think of the Many Summonses You Really Deserve—But Didn't Get." When we are stopped by an officer for some traffic violation, how do we take our medicine? Do we try to make excuses? "You see, Officer, I was in a terrible hurry." Do we insist that the policeman was overeager? "He's a new man on the force and wanted to prove that he was on the job." Do we growl about the law and say that the speed limit ought to be increased?

Some people, perhaps due to lack of humility, refuse to face the fact that they have ignored or broken a traffic law. In a way they put themselves above the law and claim immunity from penalties, although they would be the first to condemn a patrolman if he were soft with other violators. There are many millions of cars on the United States highways, and laws regulating our driving practices have been passed for our protection. The policeman who stands by my car door and writes a ticket for me is a living symbol of that protection. Paul the Apostle never drove a convertible but he did say, "Let every person be subject to the governing authorities." No Christian can ignore his advice.

O God, help us to apply our Christianity to our driving habits. If we do wrong on the highways, help us to accept reproof without anger and arrest without resentment. AMEN.

Nothing Doing Every Minute

> *For to you is born this day in the city of David a Savior, who is Christ the Lord.*
> —*Luke 2:11*

ON THE MORNING OF THE ONE-HUNDREDTH ANNIVERSARY of Lincoln's birth, a newspaper cartoon pictured two men talking on the edge of a frontier village. "Anything new?" one of them asked. "No. Nothing ever happens around here. Oh, yes, there's a new baby down at Tom Lincoln's."

Sometimes when we tell a friend about a lively vacation we've enjoyed away from home, we say, "There was something doing every minute." But often we talk about our home town in words like these: "Around here there's *nothing* doing every minute."

93

Are we not as mistaken as were the two men in Abraham Lincoln's home town? Perhaps at this moment in our city a plan is forming in the mind of a now unknown novelist for a great work of literature. Perhaps growing up with us is a boy who will become a world-renowned painter, portraying immortal scenes upon canvas. Perhaps one of our classmates is now laying the foundation of a career in science which will help him to discover the causes of cancer. These things may be happening in this place where there's "nothing doing every minute." Imagine two teenagers talking one night in the small town of Bethlehem, nearly twenty centuries ago. "What a dead town," says one. "There's never anything doing around here." And behold, that night was born a Savior who was Christ the Lord.

Open our eyes, Almighty God, that we may see the wonders of life about us. May we never despair of what thou canst do in this world, anytime, anywhere. Give us alert minds, that we may never miss a message from thee. Through Christ Our Lord. AMEN.

But My Vote Doesn't Count

> *Whoever knows what is right to do and fails to do it, for him it is sin.*
>
> *—Jas. 4:17*

"BUT MY VOTE DOESN'T COUNT," SAID THE MEMBER OF the program-planning committee of the youth fellowship, as he stayed home to watch TV. Afterward he grumbled because the year's meetings were, in his words, a flop.

"But my vote doesn't count," said one of the seniors when the choice of a graduation speaker was being made at a class meeting. So he went bowling. But how he growled when the speaker selected was dull and long-winded.

"But my vote doesn't count," said a member of the student council when the establishment of the honor system was discussed in an official meeting. So he went off for a soda in the local hole-in-the-wall. Later he howled because the matter was not settled to his liking.

Unless we take seriously our responsibilities as free citizens to express our convictions, we shall lose our freedom. Our freedom will not be stolen from us by crooked politicians; it can be lost by indifferent people—people who stay home every election day and mumble, "But my vote doesn't count." In the book of James we are told that if we know the right but fail to do it, for us it is sin. Almost all of us know that we should use our freedom to register our opinions on committees, at assemblies, and later at the polls. If we fail to do so, for us it is sin.

Eternal God, keep us from dodging our responsibilities and making excuses for ourselves when we do so. Help us to face our obligations with the determination to carry out thy will in our lives. AMEN.

Eye on the Rear-View Mirror

> *For sin will have no dominion over you, since you are not under the law but under grace.*
> —Rom. 6:14

IN A LARGE AMERICAN CITY A MAN WAS SUMMONED TO court on a traffic violation. The charge against him was dismissed when the patrolman testified: "He was driving so carefully I figured he must have done something wrong, so I stopped him." To be sure, the state trooper was a little too eager, but he understood how people behave. Here is a driver doing sixty miles an hour in a forty-five-mile-an-hour zone, all the while keeping his eye on the car's rear-view mirror. If in that mirror he sees a prowl car coming up behind him, how quickly he slows down. One minute he's a speeder; the next he's a law-abiding citizen. But he becomes an obedient citizen only because he is afraid of the law. He won't keep the law unless he's propped up by outside pressures in the form of policemen. Paul the Apostle speaks of Christians as being "not under the law but under grace." He means that a mature Christian will obey the law, not through fear of a wailing siren, a uniform, and a badge, but because he has yielded himself to Christ and has permitted Christ to become his regulator.

O God, help us to surrender the control of our lives to Christ, that he may guide and direct us in all that we do. AMEN.

No Small Towns, Only Little People

A citizen of no mean city.
—*Acts 21:39*

A LOUD-SPOKEN LUNCH-COUNTER PHILOSOPHER WAS ADvertising his empty-headed condition in a small restaurant. Said he: "Tell me what you eat, and I'll tell you what you are." At that a meek little man sitting

97

three stools away called to the waiter: "Cancel my order for shrimp salad, please." Some people are very conscious of size: if they are short in stature they worry about it; if they drive a small car they are ashamed of it; if they live in a small town they apologize for it. But size can be measured in different ways. For one thing, a person can be measured by the height and breadth and depth of his interests. We ask, "Can he see beyond his routine work and hobbies and petty projects, or is he content to stay walled-up in the shell of his minor interests?"

The size of a town can be judged by the size of the people who live in it. If the citizens of a town have far-ranging thoughts and can fling great dreams across a wide canvas, they will help to make their town great. There are really no small towns, only little people. A town is as big as the visions and aspirations of its individual citizens. Paul once spoke of himself as "a citizen of no mean city." He was a man of such great vision and mighty deeds that he would add stature to any town, however small, in which he lived.

O Father, grant that we shall never become self-satisfied and smug. Teach us how we may grow in wisdom and stature. Prepare us to take a useful place in our community and world. AMEN.

AT CHURCH

Be a Mirror, Not a Sponge

> *And the angel said to them, "Be not afraid; for behold, I bring you good news of a great joy which will come to all people."*
>
> —*Luke 2:10*

A SALESMAN IN ONE OF NEW YORK'S BIGGEST STORES SAYS that at least ninety-nine out of every one-hundred people who try out a fountain pen write their names. In explaining this the salesman said, "This is just one more proof that man's main interest in life is himself." Sometimes even Christians seem to have a vital interest *only* in themselves. Perhaps we have heard some people say, "My Christianity is a personal matter and is entirely between God and me." The members of the early Christian church knew better than this. They felt that they had to pass to "all people" the good news about the coming of Christ to the earth. To many of those who gave their lives to spread the story of God's love for men, their main interest was *not* themselves.

A Christian should not be like a sponge but like a mirror that reflects the light. The help that we get from our trust in God should be carried to other people. This is something we cannot be selfish about. If we think only about what God can do for us, then we are like cisterns in which water grows stagnant from want of motion. Rather, we should be channels through which our faith is made known to others.

We are glad and thankful for thy great love for us, O God. May we share our faith with others, passing on to them the blessings that we have received from thee. Through Christ our Savior. AMEN.

Front Seat in the Choir Loft

When I look at thy heavens, the work of thy fingers, the moon and the stars which thou hast established; what is man that thou art mindful of him?

—Ps. 8:3, 4

A YOUNG FELLOW HAD A JOB HAULING MAILBAGS FROM the railroad station to the post office. This made him a government employee. One day as he was pushed around by another workman, he said, "You be careful. When you crowd me you're crowding the United States government." A really big fellow! And there is a little of his spirit in all of us, for we may often feel that there is something special about us. For example, if we sing in our church's choir, we may be tempted to tread on other people's feet so we can get on the front row where we can be seen. If we are not in clear view—we might feel—members of the congregation may get the idea that the choir is coming apart. We might stop our shoving and jostling, if we would pause to recall that we are only one member of the choir, of the team, or of the cast.

There's a sure-fire cure for all of us if we ever should begin to get fatheaded. We might step outside the church on the night of choir rehearsal and look up. After we've counted all the stars, let us think of the Mighty One who is in charge of all that. Let us measure ourselves with our God. How tall are we, really?

Teach us, O God, how to use our talents without tramping on anybody else. Keep us from getting vain and puffed up. If we begin to feel that any group we belong to would collapse without us, then let us remember thee, the Creator and Ruler of the universe. AMEN.

Are You Oversensitive?

It is his glory to overlook an offense.
—*Prov. 19:11*

SOMEONE SAID TO AN ATTRACTIVE GIRL: "YOU ARE BEAUTI-
ful and there are so many young men who would like
to go out with you. Why are you so faithful to that
homely boy you're going with?" The girl answered:
"Because he never hurts my feelings." All of us, like
the pretty girl, try to protect our feelings. Often this
is not easy to do, because some of us are too quickly
hurt. We are oversensitive. If we see two people
whispering in a room we have just entered, we are
sure they are talking about us. If someone a little un-
ceremoniously challenges a pet conviction (or is it a
prejudice?) of ours, we are crushed. If at a committee
meeting our opinion is disregarded, we feel we've been
trampled on. Our feelings are very, very tender. The
worst of it is that we find oversensitive people in
church, in the Sunday school, and in the youth group.
Church, which should be a place where we esteem and
trust one another, seems to be the place where some of
us get hurt most often.

If we look into the mirror of our lives, and see the
reflection of a thin-skinned, touchy ego that can stand
no needling, we might listen to the author of the book

of Proverbs speak of a man whose glory is to "overlook an offense."

Keep us, O Lord, from hurt feelings that show we are thinking too much about ourselves. When we are exposed to mistreatment, some of it real, some of it imaginary, help us to rise above the self-pity that is the result of hurt feelings. AMEN.

What to Do in Case of Fire

Bear one another's burdens, and so fulfill the law of Christ.

—Gal. 6:2

A HUGE POLITICAL RALLY WAS TO BE HELD IN A CITY hall, and an official was interviewing young men who were applying for an ushering job. He asked one applicant, "What would you do in case of fire?" The youth said, "Oh, don't worry about me, I'd get out all right." And that's what religion means to some of us: "I'm a Christian, so I'm safe." If this is what we are thinking, we have misunderstood our faith. In Christianity I am my brother's keeper; that is, I am interested in him, concerned about him and responsible for him.

105

How deeply are we interested in the needs of the other young people in our church? If Bill, who has been attending fellowship meetings faithfully, is absent for four Sundays in succession, do we care enough about him to find out whether illness or trouble have come to him? "Keeping up with the Joneses" is an old phrase which describes how competitively we live. To the Christian, the expression should mean keeping *aware* of the Joneses; that is, keeping alert to them as our Christian friends. In case of fire (or disaster, or any kind of trouble) "getting out all right" ourselves is not enough. Every Christian should be our concern, for, as Paul says, we should be prepared and willing to bear the burdens of others.

We confess, O God, that so often our first, and sometimes only, concern seems to be with our own lives. Instill in us a lively interest in other people and a keen awareness of their needs. With this awareness grant to us a willingness to be used by thee in their service. AMEN.

When First Things Come Second

> *Seek first his kingdom and his righteousness, and all these things shall be yours as well.*
>
> —Matt. 6:33

THE MINUTES OF ONE OF THE SUNDAY EVENING MEETINGS of a youth fellowship read this way: "The meaning of church membership was discussed briefly. . . . After a long discussion it was moved, seconded, and carried that a badminton set be bought." Perhaps we remember some meeting of our club or fellowship when our members spent an hour discussing not the wrong thing, but the trivial thing. Often we hear that some youth fellowship is coming apart. At its poorly attended meetings nothing of consequence is discussed and nothing of importance gets done.

What about the youth fellowship *we* belong to? Do we believe enough in its value to ask a keen, wide-awake friend, who does not belong, to join it? If not, perhaps our reluctance shows that we are dissatisfied with our programs, which we have to admit are mostly trivial and trite. It could be that as a youth fellowship we let things of first importance slide into second place. But if we are willing to "seek first the kingdom of God," then we will never have a reason to be ashamed of our group.

Our Father, we pray that thou wilt help us to be

serious about important things. Help us to live close enough to thee to know what they are. Show us how to contribute our share toward making our fellowship strong and meaningful. AMEN.

Pull the Load Yourself

> *For I am not ashamed of the gospel: it is the power of God for salvation to every one who has faith.*
> —Rom. 1:16

IN LONDON, A DRAYMAN NAMED JOSEPH HAWES RENTED A pony to pull a heavy cart. When he hitched Dolly to the wagon, she refused to pull. Hawes coaxed and teased her—still no action. Disgusted, he unhitched her, tied her to the tailgate, and pulled the load himself. Some of us are always trying to get the load pulled for us. High-school students who take Latin have been found using a "pony" so they could get a free ride through a tough subject.

Often we expect the minister to pull the whole load of responsibility in our church. It is time to think about helping him. For example, we expect him to invite outsiders to become members of the church. "That's his job," we say, and forget that God expects

108

us to get into harness ourselves. To be sure, inviting our acquaintances to become Christians is not an easy task; not an easy one, but a great one. Not one of us has a right to call himself a Christian if he is ashamed to tell others of his faith. When we lead a classmate or a teammate to accept Christ as Savior, we have done one of the greatest jobs in the world. Then we have pulled some of the load ourselves.

Guide us, O God, to see that the little we can do gets done. Keep us from shifting our Christian duties to the backs of other people. May the faith that is in us be so contagious and winsome that our friends may become Christians. AMEN.

Don't Lose the Fire Hose

If you are offering your gift at the altar, and there remember that your brother has something against you, leave your gift there before the altar and go; first to be reconciled to your brother, and then come and offer your gift.

—Matt. 5:23-24

A FIFTY-THOUSAND DOLLAR FIRE WHICH BURNED A CITY block got plenty of attention from firemen, who tried their best to put it out. One fire department raced to the scene from a city twenty-eight miles away hoping to help put out the blaze, but when they arrived, they found they had lost their fire hose. The truck was there, the men were there; but how foolish they felt as they stood helpless.

After the morning service on Sundays, we go out to face the difficulties of everyday living—living that demands the best spiritual equipment. A Christian must be outfitted with a knowledge of the Bible, and eagerness to do God's will, and the habit of praying. He may have all these pieces of equipment and still be unable to worship properly. If he has cheated his neighbor, or hurt him in any way, he will need to go to that neighbor and make his peace with him. Only when right relations are established with others can our worship of God be meaningful and sincere.

Teach us the meaning of unselfish living, O God. Increase our capacity for being thoughtful and considerate of all the people we know. Grant to us the willingness to right the wrongs of our own making, and to forgive the wrongs we suffer from others. AMEN.